101
THINGS
TO DO
WITH A
BANANA

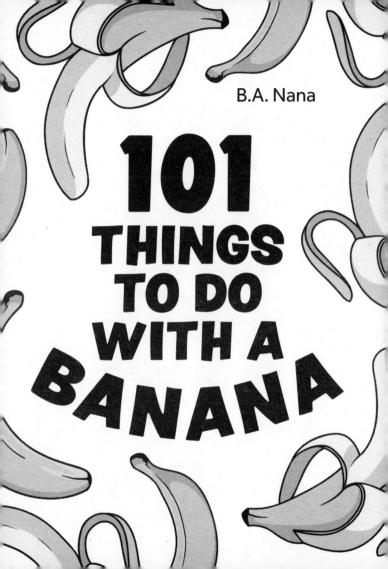

B.A. Nana

101
THINGS
TO DO
WITH A
BANANA

HarperCollins*Publishers*
1 London Bridge Street
London SE1 9GF

www.harpercollins.co.uk

HarperCollins*Publishers*
Macken House, 39/40 Mayor Street Upper
Dublin 1, D01 C9W8, Ireland

First published by HarperCollins*Publishers* 2023

10 9 8 7 6 5 4 3 2 1

Illustrations © Ollie Mann 2023

Anna Mrowiec asserts the moral right to be identified
as the author of this work

A catalogue record of this book is available from the British Library

ISBN 978-0-00-857896-1

Printed and bound in the UK using 100% renewable electricity
at CPI Group (UK) Ltd

MIX
Paper | Supporting
responsible forestry
FSC™ C007454
www.fsc.org

This book is produced from independently certified FSC™ paper to
ensure responsible forest management.

For more information visit: www.harpercollins.co.uk/green

Introduction

This book is an inexhaustive list of the many things that one might choose to do with a banana, the world's happiest fruit.

There are plenty of reasons to love this bendy yellow hero, from its inimitable taste to its serotonin-producing properties. Bananas are incredibly easy to carry around (considering they come wearing their very own body-swamping shell-suit), easily boost health and energy levels, and have myriad surprising practical uses.

A favourite with everyone from tennis players to slapstick comedians, from fussy kids to apes, the banana is the unsung champion of the fruit bowl and this book is a true celebration of its unrivalled versatility.

1.
Make banana bread – obviously

Ingredients

250g plain flour
1 tsp baking powder
½ tsp bicarbonate of soda
½ tsp ground cinnamon
½ tsp salt
110g unsalted butter
150g caster sugar
2 large eggs
2 tsp vanilla extract
3 large bananas, mashed

Method

1. Preheat the oven to 180°C/350°F/Gas 4. Grease a 900g (2lb) loaf tin.

2. Mix together the flour, baking powder, bicarbonate of soda, cinnamon and salt in a large bowl.

3. In a separate bowl, beat the butter and sugar until light and fluffy. Add the eggs and vanilla and mix well, then add the mashed banana and combine.

4. Add the dry ingredients to the wet ingredients and fold in gently, making sure not to overmix.

5. Spoon the mixture into the loaf tin and bake for about 60 minutes, or until a toothpick inserted into the middle comes out clean.

6. Allow to cool in the tin for 15 minutes, then remove to a wire rack to cool completely.

2.

Turn them into little people for your very own banana theatre

Just use a marker pen to add little faces and, if you don't fancy making your own clothes for them, Barbie outfits work well for little banana costumes.

3.
Play an old-school practical joke

NB: This author cannot be held responsible for any injury to body or pride that may incur for intended victim. For best results, perhaps position some cushions or gym mats strategically, and keep laughter to a sensitive level.

4.
Use it as a shaking-hands proxy

Very useful in flu season, or for anyone with sweaty palms.

5.

Make an all-natural face mask for an instant glow

Ingredients

1 ripe banana, mashed
1 tsp honey
3 tbsp rice flour

Method

1. Mix all three ingredients together to form a smooth paste.

2. Apply to a cleansed and dry face.

3. Leave for 15 minutes, then remove by gently massaging your face with water and wiping away the remnants with a flannel.

6.
Grab someone's attention quickly

7.

Make yourself a delicious and refreshing banana milkshake

Ingredients

1 banana
1 tbsp honey
25ml single cream
75ml full-fat milk
½ tsp vanilla extract

Method

1. Combine all the ingredients in a blender until smooth.

2. Serve in a frosted glass (or a normal one if you can't be bothered).

8.

Use the peel to whiten your teeth

The cheapest and easiest way to get a dazzling smile!

Select a ripe banana and peel off a strip of the skin, keeping as much of the inside stringy bits intact as possible. Rub the inside of the strip across the outside of your teeth, ensuring they are all coated in its paste. Leave it on for about 10 minutes – lying back will help to keep your saliva from washing it away, but try to keep your lips pulled back from your teeth as much as possible.

Then simply wash it off with your toothbrush and rinse. For best results, use once a day for two weeks.

9.
Use it as a pretend phone

10.
Make a smoothie

Bananas make for the perfect smoothie base, with a texture unique among fruits.

Whereas most fruits have large amounts of water in them, resulting in a very watery smoothie, bananas will give you the desired thick, creamy, smooth drink you're looking for. They're also deliciously sweet, so will balance any bitter or sour fruits or veg that are in the mix.

There are myriad smoothie recipes out there, but if you've got a banana included you can't go too far wrong. Just add any additional fruits or vegetables you like the taste of, potentially some yoghurt or nut butter if you have some, some seeds if you're feeling wholesome, and either some water or milk. Then blend until it's smooth (you may have guessed that – the clue is, after all, in the name).

11.

Fashion an elaborate Carmen Miranda-style headpiece

12.
Cure a hangover

If you've indulged in too many banana split martinis (see page 40), you're in luck! While bananas may have got you into this mess, they can also get you out of it. A combination of their high potassium levels, fibre and sugar will help to set you to rights again. You can either consume these as nature intended or, if you're able to drag yourself from the sofa, in one of the many delicious recipes in this book.

13.

Create everyone's favourite BBQ or campfire-friendly dessert: the banana boat

Ingredients

1 banana per person
Handful of fillings: chocolate chips, marshmallows, meringue bites or strawberries

Method

1. Split each banana lengthways, cutting through the peel and banana but not all the way to the other side.

2. Use a fork to push the banana to each side, away from the centre, to make more room for your fillings. Stuff the gap with your chosen fillings.

3. Wrap in silver foil and bake on your fire/ barbecue for 5 minutes. If you have neither, cook in the oven at 150°C/300°F/Gas 2.

4. Wait until it has cooled a little, then eat with a spoon.

14.

Reach objects that are just a little too far away

15.

Observe the passing of time – and reflect on your own mortality

With just over a week for your bananas to go from green to black, you have the perfect opportunity to muse philosophically on the transience of life and your own ephemeral imprint on the earth.

16.

Pretend you're Harry Potter

Forget unicorn hair or dragon heartstrings for wand-core ingredients – a banana surely has many more magical properties. (Plus you can always eat it as a consolation if the spell goes wrong.)

17.

Use in place of a 15cm ruler

(Assuming you can find a banana that is exactly 15cm long.)

18.

Use as a pointer for your next office presentation

This touch of whimsy will keep your colleagues much more engaged than even the flashiest laser pointer. A banana-pointer can also be used by teachers, university professors and anyone delivering a Ted Talk.

19.

Get rid of pests from your plants

It turns out not everyone loves bananas (weird, right?) and the smell of a banana peel actually is a real turn-off for aphids. So if you want to rid your greenery of these unpleasant sap-suckers, just place finely chopped banana peel around the base your plant. Any existing aphids should soon jump ship and the peel will act as a deterrent to any new ones.

To stop slugs and snails eating your precious plants, simply leave a banana skin in your flower beds, then bin it – and clinging gastropods – the next day.

20.
Play a messy game of fetch with your dog

21.

Treat acne

There are hundreds of acne treatments on the market, many claiming to have all natural, organic, non-abrasive ingredients. But there is nothing so natural as sticking a banana peel on your face. The lutein they contain is an antioxidant that will help to reduce inflammation, and with a whole host of other vitamins and minerals they will help to calm your skin and reduce acne outbreaks. Just make sure your face is cleansed and that your banana is ripe, then gently message your skin with the inside of the peel for around 10 minutes.

Eating the banana inside may very well help too.

22.
Use to stuff your bra

Why should melons and peaches have all the fun – whoever said breasts shouldn't be long, thin and bendy?

23.

Pretend to someone you're happy to see them

24.

Throw them at slow people on your way to work

Also applicable for the school run or if someone isn't paying attention in the queue for the checkout.

25.

Tap someone on the shoulder (and pretend it wasn't you)

They're much less likely to guess with the added reach a banana can give you.

26.
Get rid of DVD or CD scratches

Perhaps less useful now than in 1996.

If you have a CD or DVD with scratches that keeps sticking, you can use a banana to polish and smooth out its surface using the following method: First, rub a freshly cut banana over the entire surface of the underside of your DVD or CD, then wipe it down with the inside of the banana peel. Then wipe the entire surface again, this time with a clean cotton cloth, in a circular motion. The banana residue will remain in the cracks, meaning you'll be listening to your favourite Boyzone CD again without the disruption.

27.

Moisturise your feet and repair cracked heels

Bananas can be used on their own for this, but a fantastic remedy involves mixing one mashed ripe banana with a tablespoon of melted coconut oil. Simply apply the resulting concoction all over your feet and wait for 20 minutes before rinsing off with cold water, revealing remarkably soft and supple skin underneath.

28.

Fertilise plants

Here are no fewer than three ways (certainly not as few as two) to use banana peels in your garden:

Liquid fertiliser and pest repellent

Place a few banana peels into a large food storage container and add water so that it just covers the peels. Leave for three days, stirring occasionally. Strain the liquid off and use this to water your plants – an added bonus will be that it will deter aphids (see page 26).

Slow-release fertiliser

Cut banana peels into small pieces and dry them out in the sun on a tray – if you can't wait for the next warm, bright day, the oven will work (on a low heat with the door open a fraction). Blitz them into a powder in your blender or grind them with a pestle and mortar, then stir the powder into the soil to improve its nutritional value. Orchids, in particular, will flourish with this slow-release fertiliser.

Mulch

Simply place the banana on top of the soil around your plants (not touching the plant itself) and cover with a layer of standard mulch. As they decompose, they will release nutrients to feed your plants. As well as improving the quality of the soil they will help to discourage weeds, and provide a home for plant-friendly microorganisms and insects.

29.
Give yourself that classic 80s look

Working girl,
eat your
heart out.

30.
Polish silverware and jewellery

This simple method will have your tarnished pieces gleaming in no time.

1. Put three banana peels in a blender with a dash of water and blend to make a paste.

2. Use an old toothbrush or soft cloth and work the paste into your silver.

3. Wash off the banana by submerging in water and gently working the paste off. Pat dry with a cotton cloth.

31.
Become Mr Bananahands

Much less dangerous than Edward Scissorhands, but perhaps less effective for cutting hedges or ladies' hair.

32.

Treat puffy eyes and dark circles

If banana fun and games have kept you awake most of the night, try this remedy to reduce those telltale dark circles.

Take a banana peel and scrape out the white fibres clinging to the inside. Put these in a bowl and mix with a teaspoon of aloe gel, then smooth this mixture underneath your eyes with your fingertips (avoiding contact with the eyes themselves). After 15 minutes wipe off gently with a flannel.

33.

Make a banana split martini

Please the adult and the child inside you all in one go, with this juvenile twist on the James Bond classic.

Ingredients

150ml vodka
5 tbsp crème de cacao
5 tbsp banana liqueur
Whipped cream
Banana slices

Method

1. Combine the vodka, crème de cacao and liqueur in a shaker with some ice cubes and shake for 30 seconds.

2. Strain the mixture into a cocktail glass of your choice, add a layer of whipped cream and artfully decorate with banana slices.

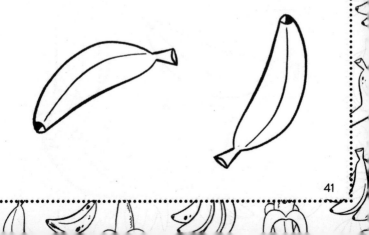

34.
**Create fancy
(temporary) jewellery**

35.
Use as very, very light hand weights

These may not build muscle tone, but you will have a healthy snack on hand as soon as you're done with your workout.

36.
Conduct the Royal Philharmonic Orchestra

A little less springy than a conductor's baton, but much more entertaining for any children in the audience.

37.

Improve your sleep quality

If the tribulations of the world are keeping you up at night, a banana may just be the answer to all your problems. Add a washed ripe banana skin to a small saucepan and cover it with a cup of boiling water. Bring to the boil and simmer for 10 minutes, then strain off the water into a mug and drink. You may wish to add a teaspoon of honey to sweeten it, or the milk of your choice.

Enjoy sweet dreams of happy bananas.

38.

Ensure a quick getaway

Pop a banana into your pursuer's car's exhaust pipe prior to said attempted getaway.

39.

Prevent inner-thigh chafing

Reportedly something Bradley Wiggins swears by ahead of long days on his bike. If you want to minimise risk of inner-thigh chafing, just rub the affected areas with the inside of a banana peel for natural lubrication. The added benefit: a pleasant aroma between your legs.

40.

Create a body scrub to exfoliate dry skin

Ingredients

1 overripe banana

2 tbsp granulated sugar

1 tsp olive oil

Method

1. Mash the banana until smooth.

2. Combine the mashed banana with the sugar and olive oil, then place the mixture in an airtight container.

3. Use up within two days and store in the fridge to prolong its freshness.

41.
Make an unsuccessful boomerang

42.

Create an edible centrepiece for your table

43.

Speed up the ripening process of an avocado

There are few things more disappointing than a hard avocado, but you don't have to suffer for too long if you have a ripe banana to hand. Simply place your unripe avocados in a paper bag with your banana (or two) and place it in a warm spot. The banana will give out the hormone ethylene and within a day or so this will encourage your avocado to soften up a bit.

44.

Make a banoffee pie

Ingredients

For the base

150g digestive biscuits
80g salted butter

For the toffee

1 x 397g tin of sweetened condensed milk
75g unsalted butter
75g light brown sugar
1 tsp vanilla extract
4 tbsp double cream
2 medium bananas

For the topping

60g icing sugar
300ml double cream

Method

1. For the base, place the digestives in a sealed bag and bash them into fine crumbs using a rolling pin. Melt the salted butter and combine with the biscuit crumbs, then press the mixture into a greased 20cm round springform tin.

2. For the toffee filling, put the condensed milk, butter, sugar and vanilla extract in a saucepan and heat slowly on a low-medium heat, whisking continuously. Gradually bring to the boil while continuing to whisk and then reduce the heat again. When the mixture turns a dark golden brown, take it off the heat and pour into a separate bowl. Whisk in the double cream and then leave to cool.

3. Slice the bananas and place them on top of your base, then pour over the cooled filling.

4. Whisk the icing sugar and cream to form stiff peaks and scoop on top of the toffee.

45.

Make the easiest baby food ever

Ingredients

1 banana

Method

1. Mash the banana.

46.
Take arty photos for your Instagram

Whether you're going for something bright and colourful, or something sultry and faintly erotic, bananas make for the best models in Instagram-friendly photoshoots. And if you're going for something high-end, be sure to capture the oh-so-arty and mysterious bendy shadows cast by said bananas.

47.

Tape it to your face in Movember

Great if you struggle to grow a moustache, or don't want the hassle of trying to keep yours neat.

48.

Easily lift stubborn ink stains from your skin

If, like King Charles III, you simply cannot stand pens that leak all over your hands just as you're signing important documents – fear not! You don't need to remove your top layer of skin by scrubbing with harsh chemicals if you have a banana to hand. Just rub the inside of a banana peel on the affected areas, wait a few minutes, then rinse off to leave your hands ink-free.

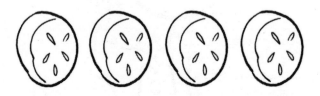

49.
Look like a pro on the tennis court

So what if you can't actually get the ball over the net and the tennis scoring system is more incomprehensible to you than trickle-down economics? Just walk around the courts wolfing down banana after banana and everyone will think you're the next Federer in training.

50.

Make elaborate toothpick art

Just mark the design of your choice across the surface of the banana, lightly breaking the skin, and as the hours go by the pattern will become more pronounced and the lines will darken. This can be a great way of writing a lovely little note in your child's lunchbox, a passive aggressive memo to a housemate, or freaking out your spouse if they take a banana to work with them – for the latter, just write a note shortly before they leave and it won't show up until later.

51.

Hang a banana painting

If you find yourself without a hammer but desperate to hang your favourite banana-themed artwork in your home, the solution is simple. Just freeze a banana until rock solid and you'll find you have a ready-made mallet.

52.
Make a natural fruit-fly trap

Famously hard to get rid of, these big-eyed bugs are a huge nuisance in the kitchen. But the best way to tackle your pernicious pest problem is a homemade, inexpensive one.

Take an overripe banana and add some of the flesh and peel to a large glass. Squirt a little dish soap on top, then add apple cider vinegar until the glass is one-third full. Lastly, blast it with hot tap water so the mixture bubbles and froths up. You'll soon find the fruit flies come buzzing over to get caught in the trap and it won't be much longer before your kitchen is fly-free.

53.

Paint it like one of your French girls

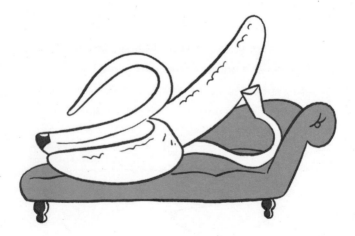

54.

Relieve common skin ailments

From bruises to skin irritations, warts to bug bites, the banana is a miracle cure-all. Just rub the underside of the peel gently against the offending area, leave as long as you're able and then gently wash off. Repeat once a day for as long as is needed. Nature is truly healing.

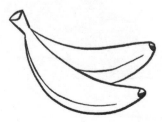

55.
Use it as a recognisable object on your blind date

I.e. 'I'll be the one with the banana.'

56.
Create your own real-life Mario Kart

57.

Make yourself some healthy banana ice cream (vegan-friendly)

Ingredients

2 ripe bananas, peeled, cut into chunks
    and frozen
2 tbsp milk of your choice
2 tbsp cocoa powder

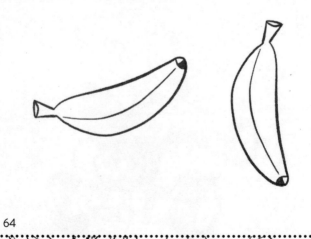

Method

1. Add all the ingredients to a food mixer and blend on high speed, scraping down the sides as needed. It may take a couple of minutes for it to run smoothly.

2. Pour into a freezer-proof container and put in the freezer until it's hard enough to scoop, but not for more than 2 hours or it will become icy.

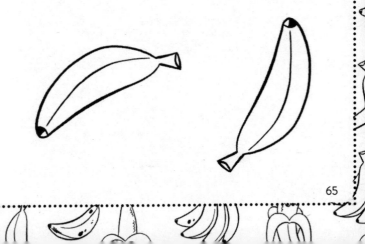

58.

Play pooh-bananas

It's like pooh-sticks, but you might be waiting on that bridge for a long time.

59.

Encourage others to start measuring in bananas

To finally overthrow the oppressive metric system.

60.

Use as a mic when the spirit moves you

If you think Celine Dion has never done this, you have another thing coming.

61.

Make banana balls, an easy no-bake snack with a funny name

Ingredients

3 bananas

400g digestive biscuits

50g desiccated coconut

Method

1. Peel and mash the bananas in a bowl.

2. Put the digestive biscuits in a sealed bag and bash them into fine crumbs using a rolling pin.

3. Combine the mashed bananas and digestive crumbs, mixing to make a thick paste.

4. Divide the mixture up into small balls – the quantity will depend on the size you choose. Roll them in your hands to make them perfectly round.

5. Spread the coconut on a baking tray, then roll your banana balls on the tray until they are coated. Put the balls into the fridge for 30 minutes until firm.

62.
Direct traffic

The time of the lollipop lady has passed. It's time to usher in the time of the banana being.

63.

Heal your haemorrhoids

Haemorrhoids are a less-than-desirable condition most of us will be faced with at some point or another, where inflamed or irritated veins around the anus cause pain or discomfort. While you could try creams, a lot of people prefer to opt for a homemade, non-chemical option, and one of the best remedies out there involves puréeing a banana peel with a tablespoon of witch hazel in a blender. Just soak a clean cloth in your homemade concoction and place it on the affected area for half an hour. You can do this once a day, or twice if you are really suffering. It should reduce swelling, pain and the telltale waddle in your walk.

64.

Make some butterfly attractors

Nothing could be more charming in your garden oasis than a plethora of beautiful butterflies. While planting certain flowers will help to attract all manner of these insects, from painted ladies to silver-spotted skippers, in autumn when food is harder for them to find, you might consider making your own attractor.

To do so, take a ripe/overripe banana and, while it's still in its peel, squeeze it with your hands. Then gently pierce the skin of the banana with a sharp knife in a few places, and squeeze the banana a little more. Place the banana on a plate or tray and leave it in a sunny spot. Butterflies love a sugary treat, so you should soon find any in the vicinity showing up to check it out.

65.
Give someone a very cheap birthday present

People are always going on about wanting Apple products – why shouldn't a banana get a look in?

66.

Make banana dolphins

The perfect offering for a kid's party (or frivolous adult party), these are so easy to make but incredibly effective.

Take as many bananas as you want dolphins and cut off the ends, at around two-fifths from the stalk. Make sure you select bananas with at least a couple of centimetres of stalk that aren't too ripe. (Don't waste the rest of the banana – why not freeze it in chunks to make the banana ice cream on page 64?)

Stand the bananas upright – if this is difficult, try cutting the bottom at a different angle. Then cut a deep slit into the stalks horizontally to form a mouth and pop a grape into the slit to mimic a beachball. Lastly, draw on eyes with a black marker pen.

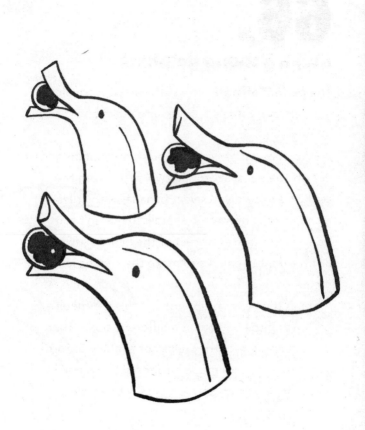

67.
Make a banana peel octopus

Another great addition to the food table at a party (decoration only), or simply as a fun activity to fill a spare half-hour on a slow weekend.

Take a banana and peel back the skin so it falls in eight equal-sized 'arms', leaving about 8cm intact at the stalk end. Prop it up so it can stand independently and draw a face onto the body with a marker pen. There are no points for realism.

Feed your pet monkey

Not just an urban legend put about by banana farmers, it really is true: monkeys love the stuff. Can't get enough of it.

Dice one and use it to play a game of Slimy Draughts

To differentiate them, stick a toothpick into each draught of one set.

70.

Play a rousing game of jousting bananas

The stakes may not be as high as they were in the medieval version of jousting on which this game is based, but that doesn't mean you can't have a cracking good time.

You will need to have two knights (for authenticity), each standing at either end of the room and facing one another, with a banana apiece (still in its peel). Upon the starting signal ('CHARGE' is particularly appropriate), they should proceed to run at one another with their banana pointed at the other knight. Unlike in the original version, your aim is not to hit your opponent with your banana, but rather to knock your opponent's banana out of their hands. The knight to achieve this is the winner and should play the next challenger until an overall winner is determined.

71.

Make beautiful (temporary) Christmas tree decorations

You will need

Small bananas
Glitter glue/tinsel/
    embellishments of
    your choice
Strong tree ornament
    hooks

Method

1. Decorate your banana with glitter or the embellishments of your choice.

2. Stick the bottom end of your hook under the stalk of your banana, ensuring you have good purchase.

3. Hang the other end of your hook on a strong branch of your tree – usually the ones at the very top are good for heavier banana-based decorations.

These will last a few days at most before they look like Halloween decorations. Actually, that's probably a better idea.

72.

Make a silent wind chime

No one wants to hear that annoying
tinkling anyway.

73.

Play a spirited game of
Hot Banana

It's like Hot Potato ... but, you know,
with a banana.

74.

Make every child's (and big child's) favourite dessert: the banana split

Ingredients

Bananas, split in half lengthways
(as many as you want)
Ice cream (as much as you want)
Chocolate sauce (as much as you want)

Method

1. Combine in any way you fancy.

#

Play a banana duelling game

The rules are simple: duellers take a banana each in their dominant hand and face each other. They must place their other hand behind their back.

   An adjudicator signifies when the duellers should begin by blowing a whistle or shouting 'BANANA'. The duellers should then race to peel their banana using only their chosen hand and then squish the banana into their opponent's face. The first person to do so is the winner.

76.
Make a dog treat

Because why should humans have all the fun?

Ingredients

  3 ripe bananas
  350g porridge oats
  3 tsp cinnamon
  1 tbsp olive oil

Method

1. Preheat the oven to 110°C /225°F/ Gas ¼.

2. Mash the banana and combine with the other ingredients in a mixing bowl. You are looking for a pliable, thick dough, so stir until you achieve the desired consistency. Cover the bowl and allow to rest for 5 minutes, during which time the oats will expand.

3. On a clean countertop, tip out your mixture and roll it to around 1cm thick. Use cookie cutters or a knife to make your desired shapes.

4. Place the shapes onto a flat baking tray and bake for 25 minutes, then turn them over and bake for another 20 minutes.

5. Turn out to cool on a wire tray.

77.

Tape one to a wall (it's art)

If you're not as cultured as some other banana fans, you may not be aware that a banana duct-taped to a wall sold for $120,000 in 2019. It was by Italian artist Maurizio Cattelan and was titled 'Comedian'.

   You may not get the same amount of money for yours, but art isn't all about the pay day.

78.

Make vegan 'pulled pork'

Ingredients

  2 bananas (pre-ripened, washed)
  1½ tbsp olive oil
  1 tsp chilli powder
  1 tsp paprika
  ¾ tsp mustard powder
  ½ tsp garlic powder
  ½ tsp onion powder
  2 tbsp vegan barbecue sauce
  Pinch of salt

Method

1. Slice the top and bottom off the washed
    bananas and remove the peel – you don't
    need the actual fruit, so you can eat them or
    use for one of the other activities in this book.

2. Scrape off the stringy white inside of the peels and discard, then cut the peel into very thin strips – you may wish to use a fork to 'shred' these off as finely as possible.

3. Cut the strips so they are around 8cm long.

4. In a bowl, coat the shredded peels in the olive oil, chilli powder, paprika, mustard powder and onion powder. Cover and leave to stand for 10 minutes.

5. Heat a saucepan on a medium heat with a splash of water and add your shredded peels. Cook for a few minutes until tender (but not mushy). It should take around 5 minutes.

6. Remove from the heat and add your barbecue sauce and salt, stirring until fully combined.

Best eaten in a bap with some coleslaw and salad.

79.

Tenderise meat

As well as making delicious vegan fare (see page 90), bananas can be used to tenderise meat. Simply add some washed and chopped peel to your marinade, or into the frying pan/dish while cooking your meat. The peel will help to break down the proteins and speed up the meat-softening process.

80.

Make sports day more fun with a rather sticky relay race

Bananas are a much easier shape to hold than a baton, anyway.

81.
Perform a mic-drop mid-conversation

Much more convincing than miming it.

82.
Stir your banana bread batter

Who needs a spoon?

83.
Create a banana maze

A bit like a hedge maze, but easier to navigate.

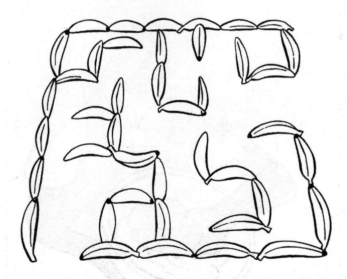

84.
Make a baby mobile

85.

Fashion yourself an ineffectual policeman's truncheon

Although if the banana is frozen, it will be more effectual (until it defrosts).

86.

Break a window

Again, freezing the banana is an important step towards making this one work. You may find a rock is quicker.

87.
Build a house

It just might not be fairy-tale-wolf-proof.

88.

Make a hair mask

If you have dry or damaged hair, bananas
are on hand to restore hydration, shine and
manageability – and even help to control
dandruff.

  Just mash up two ripe bananas and mix
with two tablespoons of honey and apply it
to slightly damp hair. You need to keep it on
for around half an hour, so covering it with a
shower cap will prevent banana stains on your
carpet – especially if you're wondering about
pretending your banana is a microphone (see
page 67). After that time, simply wash it out as
you normally would.

NB: If you're looking to encourage hair growth, you could try adding a whisked egg into the mix, but when you're washing it out make sure the water isn't too hot or you may find yourself with scrambled egg stuck in your roots.

89.

Use it to measure how deep a puddle is

This works as long as the puddle isn't deeper than the banana is long.

90.

Play a game of banana hockey

It's like real hockey, but with bananas instead of hockey sticks.

91.
Get rid of splinters

Another remarkable talent of the humble banana is its ability to draw splinters out of the skin. To allow it to work its magic, slice a small section of peel and place it with the underside against the splinter. Secure it in place with a bandage. Leave it on for a couple of hours (or overnight if the splinter is particularly wedged in there) and you should find the end of the splinter has been drawn out. Now simply use a pair of tweezers to finish the job.

92.

Grease up a slide to surprise your children

93.

Make a door impossible to open

Simply rub a round knob with the inside of the banana skin to lube it up and stand back to watch chaos unfold.

94.

Guide airplanes in to land

Most airports opt for illuminated, beacon-like marshalling wands to do this job, but the bright yellow of a banana should surely do the job just as well. Surely.

95.

Recreate the Banksy 'Pulp Fiction' artwork, in real life

All you need are two suits and two bananas. And a friend, which admittedly can be harder to come by.

96.

Reminisce about the TV show, 'Bananas in Pyjamas'

Or, alternatively, you could try putting pyjamas in bananas.

97.

Rob a bank by pretending you have a concealed weapon

Disclaimer: This author does not actually condone criminal activity, even when a banana is involved.

98.
Write a massive SOS

Useful if
you're on
an island
with lots of
banana trees.

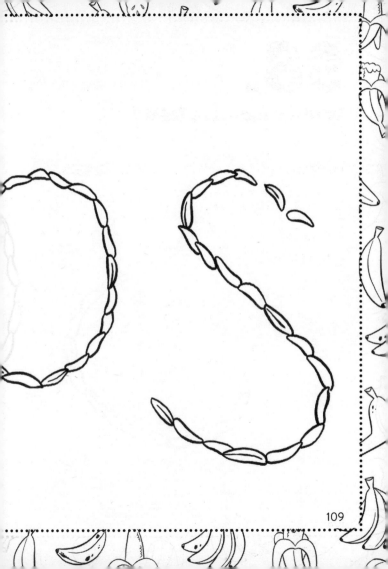

99.
Shine your shoes

Simply rub the soft inside of your banana peel all over the surface of your shoes, avoiding laces, then wipe with a dry cloth to remove the residue. Slightly green bananas will shed less but will do the job just as well.

You can try this technique on all manner of leather goods, such as wallets, bags or belts.

This will also help your leather last longer, as the potassium and natural oils are naturally nourishing. Potassium happens to be a key ingredient in commercial shoe polish, so you're just cutting out the middleman, really.

100.

Fashion a very long poking device

NB: You will need a lot of packing tape.

101.
Eat it